How to
Grow Your Food

A guide for complete beginners

Jon Clift & Amanda Cuthbert

green books

First published in 2011 by

Green Books
Dartington Space, Dartington Hall,
Totnes, Devon TQ9 6EN

Design by Jayne Jones
Illustrations by Emily Barden

ISBN 978 1 900322 68 3

Text printed on Cyclus Offset 100% recycled paper
Cover printed on 75% recycled material

Contents

Introduction

There's nothing like the taste of fruit and vegetables you have grown yourself. The flavour beats anything you will get from a supermarket and the health benefits of fresh produce that has not been stored and transported for miles, or sprayed with chemicals, are obvious. Even if you only have a windowsill or some hanging baskets you will be surprised how much you can grow - maybe there's room on a sunny stairwell or by the car park? Or if you've got a lawn, perhaps you don't need it? Grow food instead! It's fun to grow your own organic food and it saves you a lot of money.

This book will get you started: we have chosen fruit, vegetables and herbs that are easy to grow. Radishes, for example, can be grown almost anywhere in any space, are quick to give results and are relatively trouble-free compared with, say, asparagus or cauliflowers, which need more looking after and patience. There are literally hundreds of different varieties of seed available, from the tried-and-tested to the more unusual - in this book we've suggested some varieties to get you going.

It is very rewarding to eat something that you have nurtured from a tiny seed, but if you don't have much time or space you can take a short cut - many vegetables can now be bought as young plants. Where relevant we have included advice for both growing from seed and growing from a small plant that you have either raised yourself or bought.

Happy growing!

Key to symbols

 Seed   Tuber   Garden

 Plant   Container   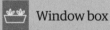 Window box

 Bulb   Indoors   Hanging basket

Chapter 1

Before you start

Before you start – a few things to think about

Space

How much space have you got? Even a tiny balcony or south-facing windowsill can be a space for growing food. Be creative – you can grow plants in pots, bags, boxes or even milk cartons. If you've only got flowerbeds, why not grow a few runner beans, some sweetcorn or a courgette or two in amongst the flowers? Herbs are really easy in containers, and as they don't need much water they also do well on sunny banks. If you have a small strip of earth by a south-facing wall (maybe down the side of a path?) grow some tomatoes – they'll like the heat from the wall. If you've just got concrete, you can grow in containers or raised beds. Whatever your space, you can grow something.

Position

Light: You'll need to think about light and shade before deciding what to grow. Most plants benefit from sunshine, so a north-facing balcony could be difficult, but maybe you have a sunny windowsill? If you have a garden, where are the sunny spots that are going to be best for growing your sun-loving vegetables? The more sun the plants get in the growing season the quicker and more productively they will grow.

Shelter: If possible, try to make sure that at least part of your growing area is out of the wind – strong winds and heavy rain can damage young plants, especially tall ones.

Weather

Be aware of the seasons where you live – you may need to adapt your growing to suit your local climate. If you live in a colder part of the country you will need to plant a bit later than if you live in the warmer south (use the later dates recommended in this book). Likewise, if you have a drier climate you will need to think about growing crops that don't mind dry conditions, or be prepared to get out there frequently with the watering can.

Soil

What kind of soil do you have? If it is thick, heavy, clay soil it is a good idea to add some compost (see page 15) to try to 'open it up' and make it less dense. If it is a light, sandy soil add well-rotted farm manure, if you can get hold of some, or compost, which will help give the soil more body and reduce water loss. Compost both adds nutrients and enriches your soil, which will mean healthier plants.

If you are growing in containers or a window box you will need a good growing compost; there are lots of different sorts on offer, but buy compost that is peat-free (let's save what peat bogs still remain!) and, ideally, organic if you can.

Water

It's a good idea to invest in some water butts to catch the free water from the roof of your house or shed; you can't have too much, especially in a dry summer. If you are running a tap in the kitchen waiting for your water to warm up, rather than waste it, collect the cold water into a bucket and save it to use it on your plants.

Equipment

You can get by with very little equipment or, in some cases, can make your own.

Tools: If you are growing indoors you can make do with an old spoon, although a trowel is handy. Outdoors you can manage with a trowel and a large fork, but a spade, hoe and rake are also useful. Garage sales are great places to find cheap tools.

Watering: A large watering can for outside; a small one or a jug for inside.

Labelling: Plant labels can be made from cut-up yoghurt pots; use a permanent marker or soft pencil.

Tying in or up: A pair of scissors and something to tie plants up with – string, thin strips of old rag, etc.

Pruning: Secateurs.

Support: Sticks, canes, trellis or netting.

Protection: Net and fleece will help to protect plants from pests and cold weather. Cloches (see page 124) are useful both for warmth and to give

Tools don't have to be new.

protection from pests; you can make your own small cloche by cutting a large plastic water bottle in half.

Containers

While you can spend a lot of money on different sorts of container, you can also find or make things to sow and grow in that cost next to nothing.

Pots and modules: There are many different kinds of container for sowing seeds in – from seed trays

Young seedlings.

and modules to pots of different shapes and sizes. You can also use yoghurt pots or fruit juice cartons (with a small hole made in the bottom), or plastic containers from supermarket-packaged fruit and vegetables.

Raised beds: You can make your own or buy ready-made ones, which are made from wood or recycled plastic, are easy to use and can be placed on solid surfaces, like concrete or gravel, or on grass or soil.

Old builders' bags: Great for larger crops such as runner beans or sweetcorn; they will need holes in the bottom for drainage.

Old baskets and buckets: Try the local recycling centre - look for buckets with holes in, or make holes yourself.

Hanging baskets: Good if you have a small space.

Window boxes: Great when space is tight.

Seeds or plants

It's fun choosing and buying seeds - there are so many to choose from. We've suggested varieties that are easy to grow, but once you have found your feet you can enjoy trying out more unusual ones.

Short on time? You can often buy young plants to avoid having to grow them from seed - where relevant we have included information on both.

Holiday cover

If you are going to be away, make sure you have someone who can look after the plants in your absence; they may need watering and/or harvesting.

Time

How much time you invest is up to you, but you will need to allow enough to cultivate your crops.

Growing in a raised bed.

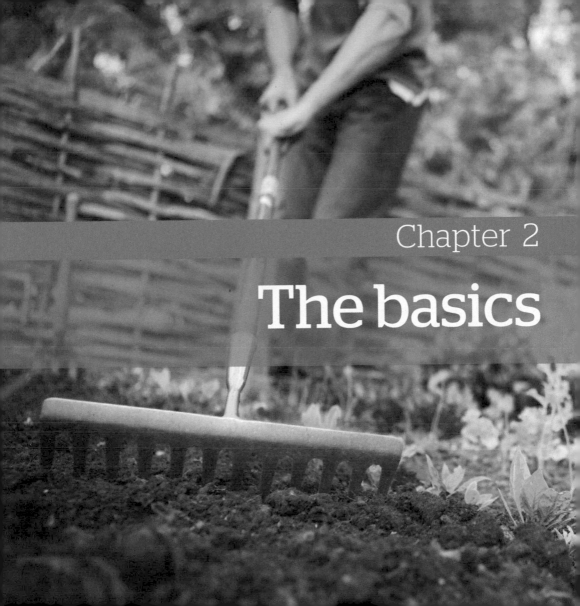

Chapter 2

The basics

The basics – getting started

You've decided where you are going to grow your food, but before you start planting you will need to get the plot ready, to give those seeds and plants every chance of success.

Your plants will need all the light they can get and food from the soil, so make wise choices now to avoid struggling plants later. Plant carefully so that your food crops are successful: for example, if you are planting amongst existing flowers, put in tall crops such as sweetcorn that will soon make their way above the flowers to reach the sun.

Clearing weeds

If you are growing in containers then skip the next few paragraphs. But if you're intending to grow on a patch of land, read on. There are some weeds, unfortunately, that really do need totally removing before you start: these are perennials that will revisit you every year unless you completely clear them away now. We're talking about easy-to-recognise weeds such as dandelions, stinging nettles and docks, as well as ones you may not know – for example, bindweed, couch grass and ground elder. Our suggestion is to find a gardening neighbour or friend who will be able to recognise these unwelcome guests – invite them round and see if they can spot any of these in your patch.

If you do have any in your patch you are going to have to get digging in order to remove all of their roots. Dandelions and docks are not too difficult but weeds such as ground elder are much more challenging. The smallest piece of root left in the ground will reshoot and grow with ease. You have to hand it to these plants – they're pretty impressive survivors.

Preparing the soil

Fingers crossed, your patch of ground is free of nasty perennial weeds. You now have a few choices:

- Dig the ground over thoroughly, breaking up big clumps of soil, whilst adding in some compost to give your plants plenty of nutrients. This is the conventional approach: hard work but very satisfying when finished.
- Clear the ground of weeds, as discussed above, roughly level off the soil and then cover it with a good depth of compost. Within reason, the more the better – but certainly no less than 7cm; double that would be great if you have enough compost.
- You can even simply dig up any perennial weeds, but leave the ordinary grass. Then cover the ground with a couple of layers of cardboard to smother the grass and prevent it growing, and

A common type of compost bin.

Buying and sowing seeds

Most of us would like to be well organised – to send off for seed catalogues months before we need the seeds, read about the various options, chat to friends who know about these things and then order our seeds for the coming season. But the reality for many of us is often a trip to the local garden centre or shop to buy what's available; in this case, be sure to check the 'sow by' date on the packet – seeds stay viable for only a limited time. Don't be tempted to buy too many – a packet of seeds goes a long way. If you have a gardening friend or neighbour then how about splitting the packets of different seeds between you?

Seeds vary tremendously in size – some even come in clusters of four or five – so you will need to use

on top of this put a good depth of compost into which you plant your vegetables.

Whatever method you decide to use, it is extremely pleasing to see your prepared bed all ready for your plants to be planted into.

Compost

You will probably need to buy in some compost (see page 124). These days it is readily available from most local authority recycling centres – they collect green waste from households and produce compost for us to use. Try to find compost that is relatively free of twigs – the less wood in it the better. Fine rather than coarse compost is preferable.

Ready to sow.

Sowing tips

- **Read what is on the seed packet** regarding depth to plant and distance apart. As a rule of thumb, cover seeds to a depth equal to their diameter.

- **Don't be tempted to plant seeds closer together than recommended:** you could end up with just a few thin, scraggly plants.

- **Sow small seeds on days when it's not too windy.**

- **If starting seeds off inside, in trays or modules, you will need to cover them with glass or a plastic bag** to keep them moist and then put them in a warm, draught-free place to germinate. (See individual plant entries for information on sowing indoors in containers or planting direct into the ground.)

different methods when it comes to actually sowing them.

For small seeds, take a 'pinch' of them between your finger and thumb, rubbing your finger and thumb together to release them into the drill or furrow (see page 125) – as gentle rain rather than a sudden downpour. Cutting a corner off the packet and gently tapping never seems to work very well.

Although seeds are relatively cheap, buying lots of different varieties adds up – so if you're after a few broad beans or a different type of lettuce, see if you can swap your extra seeds with another gardener. Contact your local allotment association or gardening club – they are generally helpful, especially to newcomers to the gardening world.

Buying and planting plants

There are several options available to you when buying plants:

Loose plants: Some of the hardier plants are sold as bunches, young leeks being a prime example. They will be cheaper this way, but do check to see that they are fit and healthy and not wilted.

A tray full of growing plants: A good option, providing it has the number of plants that you're looking for. But it is not without its drawbacks – the roots of the plants will need untangling before transplanting and some may get damaged in the process.

Plants growing in separate modules: Each plant has its own little home, which makes it very easy to transplant. Hold the tray of modules upside down, keeping one hand on the compost, tap gently to remove each plug of compost with its plant, and plant it into its new home.

Plants grown in containers made of cardboard or coir: These are sometimes known as 'plugs' and have big advantages. Simply soak well to soften up the container and, leaving the plant in its container, put it into the ground and water it in. Being biodegradable, the container will rot, allowing the roots to penetrate into the soil.

Just like seeds, plants have varying planting requirements: plant them too deep and they might rot; too shallow and they will not thrive. Follow the advice we have given in each individual plant entry. Firm down the soil around them afterwards and water them in.

A tray of young plants.

Buying tips

- **Choose plants that look healthy** – short and stocky rather than long and lanky.
- **Think twice before buying or accepting plants from friends or neighbours.** You don't want to be importing diseases or perennial weeds into your garden!
- **Your new plants will need looking after as soon as you get them.** They won't be happy being stuck in a hot car for the day while you go shopping!
- **When you get them home, water them well** and continue to nurture them until you're ready to plant them into their final home.

Watering

Your seeds and plants need water in order to grow and thrive. If they're planted outdoors in a garden, hopefully they will get the majority of their water from rainfall, but in dry periods it's down to you to provide the water.

When seedlings start growing

When your seeds in seed trays have germinated and started growing, producing both leaves and roots, they will need transplanting into separate pots or modules to give them more space. This is

Watering tips

- **Young seeds growing indoors in seed trays or modules do not require a lot of watering.** Their compost just needs to be kept damp – too much water will kill them.

- **Whenever you sow seeds or plant plants remember to water them in** – unless the compost or soil is damp already.

- **Both seeds and plants are best watered with a small watering can with a 'rose'.** This is an attachment to the spout which makes a fine rain of water – similar to a small shower head – and is gentler on seedlings. This way you won't wash away the seeds or damage young plants.

- **If possible, water early in the morning rather than the evening.** There will be less of a temperature difference between the water and soil then, so the plants won't get such a shock. This will also make conditions less easy for slugs and snails, which prefer damp soil to move across but tend to hide away during the day.

- **If you are growing plants indoors** – tomatoes, for example – try to adopt a regular pattern to your watering time. You'll find it much easier to see and know how much water is needed.

known as 'pricking out' and normally happens once the seedling has several sets of leaves (see individual plant entries for specific advice).

Get your pot ready before you start: fill it with compost, dampen the compost with water and make a hole large enough for the seedling to drop into. Your finger is a good tool to use for this.

Choose the stronger-looking seedlings. Hold the seedling gently by the leaves (not the stem), loosen the soil around its roots with a table fork, a pencil or

Seedlings growing.

something similar, and pull gently. Once the plant is free of the soil, let its weight rest on the fork and put it into its new home, still carefully holding on to it by its leaves.

Put the seedling into the hole at the same depth as it was before. Firm the compost down gently around the seedling and water it in.

Moving the growing plants to their final location

You will need to do this if you are raising plants in pots, modules or a seedbed - refer to the specific plant entry in this book to find out when and how.

Thinning out

Some plants that have been sown directly into their final position will need thinning out - removing some of the seedlings to give the rest enough space to grow successfully. This is easy with plants such as carrots or turnips: you simply grab them by their leaves and pull. But for others, such as leeks, it is more difficult as their root systems tend to become entwined. In this case you will need to gently loosen the soil around their roots with a small hand fork before pulling the unwanted plants out - hold them by their stems and tease the roots apart.

Whatever the type of plant, leave in the strong, healthy ones and remove and discard the weak.

Feeding

All plants need nutrients in order to grow and thrive. For some, such as purple sprouting broccoli, you can supply them when preparing the bed before you plant, but for others, such as tomatoes, you will need to feed the plants regularly through-out their growing season in order to get a good crop.

Rotation

To avoid the possibility of pests and diseases building up in the soil, it is a good idea not to grow the same type of crop in the same place year after year. So, where you planted carrots one year, plant courgettes the next, and so on. If you are growing in containers, change the compost every year. The obvious exception to this is perennial plants – which grow in the same spot for 15-20 years, so do not need moving around the garden. The crops in this book that are perennials are: all the fruit, rosemary, mint, sage and thyme.

Tips for moving plants

- **Get everything ready beforehand** so that vulnerable young plants do not have to be out of the soil for long.
- **Try to avoid disturbing the roots.**
- **Water in well afterwards.**

Feeding

Adding compost: For the majority of plants, mix compost into the soil before planting. As the plant grows, put more compost on top of the soil, where it will both smother weeds and be taken down into the soil by worms. This is known as 'mulching'. If you have chosen to grow your plants in compost only (see 'Preparing the soil', page 14), they will get all the nutrients they need from the compost.

Liquid feeding: If you are growing crops that require additional feeding, for example tomatoes, you will need to feed them regularly. This is done quite simply by adding some liquid feed to the water every week or so before watering; you can buy liquid feeds from garden centres or supermarkets. Buy a couple of litres; it's much cheaper this way. Just follow the instructions on the label, and don't be tempted to feed plants more than instructed – you won't get more tomatoes!

Adding compost.

Fertiliser: This comes in many forms, from chemical granules to seaweed extracts. Follow the instructions on the container.

Chapter 3

Easy-to-grow vegetables

Beansprouts

Beansprouts are the ultimate high-speed vegetable to grow. They grow easily in just a few days – no garden, no wellies, no dirty hands. Beansprouts are tasty and bursting with vitamins and minerals.

Plant or seed?

Seeds only – you're going to harvest and eat them before they grow into plants. Mung beans are easiest, but you can also try lentils, alfalfa, fenugreek and radish. But beware – you must buy special seeds or beans to sprout, as these will not have been treated with fungicides or similar, unlike the seeds and beans purchased for planting in the garden.

Sowing seeds

When and where: Beansprouts can be grown all year round, almost anywhere indoors. They've even been grown in plastic bags in explorers' pockets, but for growing at home a small jar or bowl is fine.
How: Place enough beans in the jar to cover the bottom to about two beans deep, cover with cold water and leave to soak overnight. Drain, rinse the beans, drain again and leave.

How do beansprouts grow?

After a couple of days you will see the sprouts emerging from the beans – you eat the whole lot, the bean and its sprout. Different beans and seeds will sprout in a variety of colours and sizes.

Looking after your beansprouts

Rinse and drain: All sprouting beans and seeds need frequent rinsing and circulating air to prevent them from going mouldy. Rinse and drain twice a day; the beans need to be kept moist rather than wet. A piece of loose-weave cloth held over the jar mouth with an elastic band makes draining easy.
Remove unsprouted beans: When the beans have started to sprout it is worth tipping them into a sieve or colander and removing the few that have not sprouted before returning the rest to their container.

Harvesting

When: They will be ready in just 3-5 days! If you leave them too long, roots will start to appear.
How: Just empty them out of their container.

Now what?

Clean the jar well and refill ready for the next batch.

✱ **Beansprouts will store in the fridge for several days.** Do try fenugreek and radish sprouts – they are wonderfully spicy!

Beetroot

Beetroot is easy to grow and can provide a good tasty crop early in the year. But pick it early, before the beets get tough, and try eating their tasty young leaves – they're great in salads.

Plant or seed?

Grow beetroot from seed – it is so easy and quick to grow. Choose 'Bolthardy' or, for something just that little bit different, try 'Forono', which is cylindrical rather than the normal round shape.

Sowing seeds

When and where: You can sow the seeds outdoors any time from April right up to the end of June in a sunny spot.

How: Use your finger or a stick to make a row of holes about 1-2cm deep and about 10-15cm apart, dropping a seed in each. If you're putting in more than one row, the rows need to be about 30cm apart. If planting in containers, plant seeds about 15cm apart. Water well after sowing.

How does beetroot grow?

The purple-and-green leaves start popping out of the soil after a couple of weeks, with the edible beetroot root growing quietly under the soil, gathering size and flavour.

Looking after your beetroot

Water: Young beetroots need watering regularly; this will prevent them getting tough.

Weed: The colourful leaves make it easy to distinguish the beetroot from the weeds.

Thin out: Beetroot seeds are actually clusters of about four seeds, so when the plants are about 5cm high you will need to thin them out, leaving just the strongest behind. Simply pull up the weaker plants.

Harvesting

When: 5-10 weeks after sowing seeds. Harvest early rather than late – you'll be able to see the top of the swollen root (the part you eat) appearing at soil level. Harvest them as soon as they are big enough to eat – about the size of a golf ball.

How: Hold the base of the leaves and pull gently. You might need a fork if the soil is hard.

Now what?

You can plant summer lettuce after early sowings of beetroot.

✳ **Water the plants frequently – they'll repay your kindness.** And don't forget you can add the colourful and tasty young leaves to salads.

Broad beans

Home-grown broad beans cooked and eaten soon after being picked are delicious, melting in your mouth – so unlike the tough ones found in some shops. One of the first vegetables to plant in the spring, they are easy to grow and prolific croppers.

Plant or seed?

Although broad beans are certainly cheaper to grow from seed, if you only need a few, buy some plants in April. Try 'The Sutton' if growing in a small space or 'Hylon' if you have more room.

Sowing seeds

When and where: If you are starting them off indoors, sow in January/February. Sow outdoors in early spring – March and April– ideally in a sunny spot.

How: Indoors, 1 seed to a small pot filled with peat-free compost; water lightly and label them. **Outdoors,** about 4cm deep and 20cm apart, either in rows about 60cm apart or in groups, depending on the space available.

Planting plants

When and where: Plant your plants out in a sunny spot during April.

How: Make a hole large enough to accommodate the roots and put the plants in slightly deeper than they were before. Firm down well.

How do broad beans grow?

The bean plants grow with a single main stem with leaves, and flowers then appear that turn into the

Broad bean seeds.

Broad bean flowers.

beans. The bean pods stick out from the main stem and are very visible. If growing dwarf plants, such as 'The Sutton', they will grow to a height of about 70cm. The larger varieties such as 'Hylon' will grow to a height of 1.5m.

Looking after your broad beans

Water: Garden-grown beans will only need watering in dry weather – give them a good soaking. Container-grown beans need daily watering once established.

Weed: Bean plants need most weeding when small. Once growing well they will tend to smother weeds.

Pinch out: The growing tips need pinching out once the plants reach their maximum height. You can eat these tips if you boil them briefly – they are delicious.

Support: Larger bean plants need supporting – push in stakes at either end of the row or at regular intervals around the plants, and surround the plants with string tied to the stakes.

Look out for: The tips of the growing bean plants attract blackfly (see page 130). Pinching the tips out helps prevent this infestation, although dwarf varieties generally escape the pest.

Harvesting

When: The beans will be ready in 3-4 months and can be harvested at various stages of their growth. Pick them when the pods are 5-7cm long, boil and eat whole, or wait until the pods are plump and full of beans then split them open to get the beans. Don't wait too long or the beans will become tough and leathery.

How: Grasp the main stem of the bean plant with one hand and pull the bean pod downwards to break it free with your other hand.

Now what?

Once you have harvested all the beans, pull up the plants and put on the compost heap or cut off the stems and leave the roots in the ground (bean roots contain nutrients that feed the soil).

Harvested broad beans.

You can save seeds for next year by leaving some pods on the plant until they are brown and dry. Then open the pods, take out the seeds and store in an envelope in a cool, dry place.

Carrots

There's nothing like home-grown fresh carrots, raw or cooked – the sweetness and smell beats anything from a shop and they come in all shapes and colours.

Plant or seed?

Carrots are grown from seed in rows or blocks and then thinned out. Early varieties grow quickly – try 'Early Nantes' or 'Amsterdam Forcing'.

Sowing seeds

When and where: You can sow early carrots every couple of weeks from late March through to early July. They like a sunny site and can also be grown in containers – the shorter varieties can be grown in a box. You can even grow a few in a pot on a windowsill.

How: Carrots need soil free from stones. Sow as thinly as possible to reduce the need to thin the plants later. Sow seed 1-2cm deep in rows 3cm apart with 15cm between rows, or as thinly as possible in a container. Water the seeds after sowing.

How do carrots grow?

Carrots grow below the soil, with fine frond-like leaves above.

Looking after your carrots

Water: Carrots grow best if they are watered regularly, especially during a dry spell.

Weed: Regular weeding is essential to leave room for the carrots to grow.

Thin out: Early seedlings should be thinned to 3cm apart - you can't replant the thinnings.

Look out for: Carrot fly (see page 131).

Harvesting

When: Your first carrots will be ready after 7-9 weeks, between May and July. If you prefer baby carrots, pull them up young.

How: See how big your carrots are by removing some soil from around the top with your finger. To harvest, grip the stem close to the soil and gently pull the carrot out. Try to avoid disturbing the other carrot plants if they are still too small to pick.

Now what?

Sow a second crop if you have harvested the first by the end of May.

✸ **Try not to disturb the growing plants when you are thinning out, as they will release a scent which attracts the carrot fly.**

Courgettes

Courgettes are easy to grow and great value. They come in many different varieties – yellow, round, stripy, trailing and bush. They take up a lot of room – especially the trailing variety – so if you haven't got much space try growing a bush variety. One plant will give you plenty of courgettes.

Plant or seed?

You can either start your courgettes off from seed indoors, planting out after about 6 weeks, or sow seed direct into the ground in late May. You can also buy plants, which can go straight into the soil. You'll get lots of courgettes from each plant. Try 'Defender' or, for a container, a bush variety – 'All Green Bush'.

Courgette seeds.

Sowing seeds

When and where: Sow in April in pots indoors on a sunny windowsill, or late May/early June outdoors in a sunny spot.

How: Indoors, sow one seed to a small pot, ideally planting the seed on its side to prevent rotting. Don't let the pot dry out.

Outdoors, in the ground: make a small mound and add some compost to it if you have some. Plant the seed in the middle, 3cm deep, and cover with soil; the mound will help keep the soil free-draining and so help prevent rotting. Allow 90cm between seeds/plants – the plants get very big. If planting in a container outdoors, raise the soil in the middle before planting your seed.

Planting plants

When and where: Plant your seedlings or bought plants outside when there are at least three leaves on the plant – towards the end of May or once the risk of frost is past. Courgettes grow best in full sun.

How: Plant as for seed, on top of a mound of soil. Dig a small hole with a trowel and put the plant in to the same depth as before, firming round the base.

Courgette flowers.

How do courgettes grow?

Courgettes throw out large leaves and then bright yellow flowers which turn into tiny courgettes; the longer you leave them the bigger they grow and at the height of summer you can almost see them growing, they are so fast! Before you know it they end up as marrows, so pick them small, when they are most tasty. Pick frequently to encourage the plant to produce more; if you let a courgette turn into a full-sized marrow you'll get fewer courgettes on the rest of the plant.

Looking after your courgettes

Water: They need lots of water, especially if growing in a container.

Look out for: Slugs and snails (see page 131).

Harvesting

When: Any time from July onwards once they are big enough to eat, depending on how large you like them.

How: Cut the courgette from the plant close to the main stem with a sharp knife, taking care not to nick the remaining stems.

Now what?

Once it gets colder and your plant has stopped producing, pull the whole plant up and put it in the compost bin.

Young courgette plant in a flowerbed.

✳ **Put straw underneath the plants once courgettes start to appear, to stop them getting too wet and rotting if you have a lot of rain.**

French beans

French beans are a great crop to grow as they produce lots of beans in a short amount of time, and all in a small space; they also come in many different fun colours. (Be sure to cook them before eating – they contain a toxin that must be destroyed first by cooking.)

Plant or seed?

French beans are very easy to grow from seed, but if you only want a few plants to put in a container you can buy them. Our favourite is 'Purple Teepee' – the dark purple bean pods look great and are easy to find when picking, but sadly they turn green when cooked!

Sowing seeds

When and where: Sow indoors in May; outdoors between the end of May and the end of June, in a warm sunny spot.

How: **Indoors,** sow 4cm deep, 1 seed to a small pot filled with peat-free compost.

Outdoors, about 4cm deep and about 30cm apart; if you want to sow them in rows, make the rows about 60cm apart. If you want to grow them as a group rather than in rows, plant 40cm apart. Just remember to give yourself enough space to get in and pick the beans.

Planting plants

When and where: Buy your plants or plant your own out from the beginning of June onwards, after all risk of frost is past. Plant out in a warm sunny spot.

How: Use the same spacing as for seeds. Plant to the same depth as before, gently covering the roots with earth. Press down using your hands and water well after planting.

French bean seeds.

Young French bean plant.

How do French beans grow?

They will grow about 30-40cm high, producing many flowers, which turn into the edible bean pods about 6-15cm long.

Looking after your French beans

Water: Garden-grown beans will only need watering in dry weather - give them a good soaking, especially once the pods start to form. Container-grown beans need watering daily once established.

Weed: French beans need weeding, especially when small, but once growing well they will tend to smother weeds.

Support: If they are planted in rows, some twigs stuck in the ground beside the plants will support them while they grow. Small groups of French beans will tend to be self-supporting.

Look out for: Low bean pods might touch the soil and get eaten by slugs. Weed-free soil gives the slugs nowhere to hide!

Harvesting

When: French bean pods can be harvested as soon as you can see them. However, try waiting until the pods are 6-15cm long if you can, but don't leave them too long or they will become tough and stringy. Pick frequently to keep the beans coming.

How: With one hand hold the bean plant just behind the beans you want to harvest; with the other, grasp the bean pod and carefully break it off the plant stem.

Now what?

Once your plants have stopped producing new beans, pull them up and put on the compost heap or cut off the stems and leave the roots in the ground, where they will slowly rot and feed the soil.

Row of French bean plants.

✳ You can save seeds for next year by leaving some bean pods on the plants to grow fully and dry out. Then open the pods, remove the beans, dry completely on a sunny windowsill and store until next year in a cool dry place.

Garlic

Garlic is really easy to grow. It also stores well and doesn't need much space in your garden or container. It's great to have your own string of garlic hanging in the kitchen ready to use.

Plant or seed?

Garlic is grown from garlic cloves. You can either buy them in the greengrocer or supermarket or, if you want to choose a particular variety, buy from a garden centre or catalogue. Try 'Solent Wight' or, for roasting, 'Elephant Garlic', which is larger and milder.

Planting cloves

When and where: You can plant garlic from October to February but will get larger bulbs from cloves planted between October and December. Garlic likes a sunny spot, in a light soil either in a container or in the ground.

How: Take a bulb of garlic and split it into cloves. Make a row of small holes 10cm apart (using a dibber is easiest – see page 42)) and plant one clove just below the surface in each, with the root end downwards. Cover with soil. If you plant more than one row, space the rows 30cm apart.

How does garlic grow?

Garlic takes a long time (7-8 months) to grow but can withstand winter weather. Thin green shoots appear above the ground and these gradually get taller and fatter until they are about 30cm tall. The purpley-white bulbs that you eat grow under the soil and their tops can be seen just on the surface.

Looking after your garlic

Weed: Keep the ground free of weeds between the plants.

Look out for: Birds (see page 130) – they love to pull out the new shoots.

Harvesting

When: The bulbs are ready when the leaves turn yellow.

How: Harvest the bulbs by gently pulling them or digging them up with a fork. If it is warm and sunny, lie them on the soil to dry – if not they can be dried indoors.

Now what?

Once they are dry, hang the bulbs somewhere cool and dry until you need to use them – they should keep for a long time.

✱ **Save one or two of your fattest bulbs for planting the following year.**

Leeks

Leeks are a good choice as they rarely fail, are easy to grow and give you fresh vegetables when little else is growing in the garden during the winter months.

Plant or seed?

As with most vegetable varieties, plants will be available to buy if you want. However, leeks are very easy to grow from seed. The most famous variety is 'Musselburgh'.

Sowing seeds

When and where: From late March to April outside in a small seedbed or container, somewhere where they will get the spring sun.
How: Sow the seeds as thinly as possible, about 1cm beneath the soil, or sow two seeds per small pot or module.

Planting plants

When and where: Plant in June. If buying plants, look for leeks that are about the thickness of a pencil. If transplanting from your seedbed or module, do so when the plants are about 20cm tall. Your leeks are going to be in this space for up to a year, so choose somewhere where they can grow undisturbed and will catch some winter sun.
How: Use a fork to gently lift the small leeks from their seedbed – watering the seedbed the day before you intend digging them up helps to loosen

the soil around their roots. Leeks are best planted every 15cm in rows 30cm apart, to help you with weeding later in the year. They are extremely easy to plant out: make a hole about 15cm deep by pushing a pointed piece of wood or dibber (about 4-5cm diameter) into the ground, removing it and

A dibber!

Leeks growing.

the part above the soil green. Both parts are edible, but despite this many shops remove the majority of the green leaves before displaying the leeks – what a waste!

Looking after your leeks

Water: Leeks are very robust and will survive most variations of climate, although they will definitely be bigger and juicier if watered during dry conditions. Leeks in containers will, of course, need regular watering.

Weed: Weed regularly. A hoe will fit neatly between the rows.

Look out for: Leek rust (rusty looking spots) on some leaves. There is no treatment for it, so it is best ignored. Just cut these bits off before eating.

Harvesting

You can loosen the earth around the leeks and pull them up to cook and eat whenever you want – but the longer you leave them the bigger they'll get (within reason!). They are normally ready from around December to March. Don't let them go to seed; you can easily spot this – a solid shoot starts to emerge from the centre of the plant. If this happens, dig up and use straight away.

Now what?

When you've harvested all of your leeks you can prepare the ground ready for spring, the busiest time of the gardening year – you'll need all the space you can get!

dropping the small leek plant, root first, into the hole. Water well. There is no need to fill the hole with soil.

If growing in a container, choose a large one. Fill with compost and plant as above. If space is limited the leeks can be planted about 10cm apart – but you won't get such large leeks.

How do leeks grow?

The leeks simply grow into bigger plants, with the part of the leek beneath the soil being white and

Harvested leeks.

✳ Try using leeks fresh in salads instead of onions. They are great in coleslaw – wash well, then slice both the green and white part of the leek thinly before adding to the other ingredients.

Onions

It feels good to cook with your own onions – you can never have too many and they store easily. Squeeze them in to your growing space wherever you can.

Plant or seed?

Whilst you can grow onions from seed, the easiest way is to buy 'sets' – baby onions that grow into much bigger ones. Try the yellow 'Ailsa Craig' or, if you like red onions, 'Red Baron'.

Planting sets

When and where: Plant in well-drained soil in a sunny position in March or April. They can also be grown in containers outside.

How: Make a small hole with the tip of a trowel and plant the sets 2cm deep, 10cm apart, with the roots downwards, leaving the tip just showing above the ground. Space the rows 25-30cm apart. Firm the soil round each set.

How do onions grow?

Onions produce green tips above the ground and the edible bulb grows under the soil. The green tip grows about 30cm tall and the top of the bulb starts to show slightly above the ground. When fully grown most of the onion will be above soil level.

Looking after your onions

Water: Onions need regular watering, but take care not to overwater - they can rot if you do.

Weed: Keep the ground weed-free.

Look out for: Birds (see page 130) - cover planted sets with netting to keep them away.

Harvesting

When: About 12 weeks after planting the sets, between June and September, once the leaves start to go yellow.

How: Gently loosen the roots and lift the bulbs out of the soil - if it is sunny lay them on their sides to dry for a few days; if not, bring them in to a cool dry place and dry them there, ideally on racks.

Now what?

Once your onions are dry, plait them into strings and hang up to store somewhere cool and dry.

❋ **Grow your onions in a different place each year – this will help avoid the build-up of any disease in the soil.**

Parsnips

The parsnip is one of those wonderful vegetables that will sit in the soil throughout winter just waiting to be dug up and cooked. They even benefit from a heavy frost – it makes them sweeter.

Plant or seed?

Use fresh seeds only – old seeds will not produce parsnips. 'White Gem' is a variety that is resistant to a rusty-brown discolouration called canker.

Sowing seeds

When and where: Sow the seeds from mid-April to mid-May. Parsnip seeds take a while to germinate, so expect a wait of about a month before you see their green shoots appearing.

How: Sow the seeds in rows about 2.5cm deep. Because it takes 3-4 weeks for the shoots to appear they can get lost amongst weeds. A good idea is to mix the parsnip seeds with some radish seeds, as the radishes grow quickly and act as a marker for your parsnips. Plant a bunch of radish seeds nearby so you know what their leaves look like.

How do parsnips grow?

The leaves appear first and grow about 30-40cm tall. The white root, which is the edible part, remains hidden until you dig it up when harvesting.

Looking after your parsnips

Water: Young parsnips need regular watering.

Weed: Your parsnips will need weeding regularly, especially when they are small.

Thin out: When the young parsnips have 3-4 leaves showing, remove some of the plants, leaving about 10-15cm space between the remaining ones.

Harvesting

Your parsnips will probably be ready to dig up and eat from October (scrape away the soil at the top of the plant with your hands to see if they are big enough for you!) but they will become sweeter if they are exposed to some frost. They can remain in the soil all winter, but when springtime arrives and they start shooting out new leaves you will need to dig up what's left.

Now what?

Once you have harvested all your parsnips, the ground is ready for spring planting.

✴ **If your first attempt with parsnips results in strange-shaped roots, do not despair – they will still taste wonderful!**

Peas

Peas are really easy and quick to grow; they can be grown in a container, raised bed or garden plot. Most pea varieties need support from sticks or netting.

Plant or seed?

You can grow peas from seed indoors for planting out later, or sow seed direct into the soil outdoors, or in containers, or buy plants that are ready to plant outside. Try 'Feltham First', or the dwarf variety 'Kelvedon Wonder'.

Pea seeds.

Sowing seeds

When and where: Sow February/March onwards in pots indoors or March–July outdoors in containers or your garden. They like sun or part shade.

How: Indoors, three seeds to a small pot, filled with peat-free compost. Sow 3cm deep. Put them in a sunny spot.

Outdoors, sow 3cm deep and 8cm apart with 60cm between the rows. Sow at 2-3-weekly intervals for a steady supply throughout the summer.

Planting plants

When and where: Once your indoor-grown plants are about 4cm high, and the risk of frost is past, in April or May.

How: Harden off (see page 126) your indoor-grown plants before planting outside in the ground, 8cm apart, in rows 60cm apart. Or you can grow them individually in a flowerbed. Plant to the same depth as before. Water after planting.

How do peas grow?

Peas grow in pods on vines above the ground and are usually supported by sticks or netting, which they cling to with tiny tendrils; they have attractive

Pea seedlings.

Support: Each pea plant needs supporting once it is around 8cm high, with 90cm-high canes, thin sticks or a row of netting. Their tendrils will curl round the support, but if necessary tie the plants to the support to start with. (Make sure the support is tall enough – check the seed packet for maximum plant height.)

Pinch out: Once the plants have got to the top of the supports pinch out the tops; these pea tips can be added to salads for variety.

Look out for: Mice (see page 131) – they love pea seeds; birds (see page 130) – you may need to protect plants with fleece or netting; caterpillars (see page 131) and pea moth (see page 131).

Harvesting

When: 10-12 weeks after planting seeds, from June onwards. Peas are ready to pick when the pods are round and full; harvest from the bottom of the plant first.

How: Hold the main stem and gently pull the pod from it, splitting it open to get at the peas. If you pick regularly you will encourage new growth.

Now what?

When you have harvested your peas, cut the vines off at ground level and put them in the compost/recycling bin, leaving the roots in the ground (pea roots contain nutrients that feed the soil).

flowers that become the pea pods and each pod has about six peas inside it.

Looking after your peas

Water: In dry weather, water regularly once flowers appear.

Weed: Keep weeds down.

Pea flowers.

✳ Leave a few pea pods on the vine until they dry out, remove the dry peas and save them somewhere cool and dry for next year – free seeds!

Perpetual spinach

Perpetual spinach is not really perpetual as it doesn't continue indefinitely. However, it is easy to grow and you can go on picking leaves for a long time. Our favourite kind of spinach for the garden!

Plant or seed?

Because it is easy to grow we suggest you start from seed. See if you can find the 'Popeye' variety.

Sowing seeds

When and where: Sow seeds any time from March to July in a sunny spot.

How: About 2cm deep, either in rows about 45cm apart or in groups.

How does spinach grow?

Strangely enough, these plants are a type of beetroot, but you only eat the leaves. These leaves can grow quite large – up to 45cm long and 15cm wide – and tend to look very impressive!

Looking after your spinach

Water: The seeds and small seedlings need regular watering, but once they are established they are quite hardy.

Weed: When the plants are small they will need weeding occasionally. The seedling leaves will appear quite quickly, making your task of differentiating between the spinach and the weeds easier.

Thin out: Remove some seedlings so there is about 30cm between each plant. Don't be tempted to grow them any closer together or the leaves may get mouldy.

Harvesting

When: 7-8 weeks after sowing seeds you can start picking leaves.

How: Pick from the outside of the plants, breaking off the leaves by bending them down and twisting. Leave the new inner leaves to grow, but don't allow the outside leaves to grow too large or the plants will stop producing new leaves. If necessary, pick off the large leaves and put them on the compost heap.

Now what?

Perpetual spinach will continue producing new leaves right through the summer and may continue until the following spring, if you continue harvesting the outside leaves.

✱ **To cook the larger leaves, cut up the central stem of the leaves into short lengths and cook for a few minutes longer than the rest of the leaves.**

Potatoes

Potatoes are easy to grow, don't need much attention or any support, and their roots are great for breaking up heavy soil ready for a different vegetable crop next year. The first harvest of buried treasure is always a high point in our gardening year.

Plant or seed?

Potatoes are sold as tubers – seed potatoes – not seeds or plants. There are many different varieties, shapes and colours to choose from, but early potatoes grow the fastest. Try 'Orla' or 'Sharpes Express'.

Chitting

Buy your seed potatoes in January/February. You will see little buds ('eyes') in the potato; lay the potatoes in egg boxes or on a tray with the eyes facing upwards, in a dry, light place indoors – this is known as 'chitting' (see page 124). After 3-4 weeks the eyes will sprout and the potatoes are ready to plant in the ground.

Planting

When and where: February/March, once the chitting potatoes have started to sprout. Plant outdoors in the ground or in a container. They grow best in a sunny spot.

How: In the ground, dig a trench, or make holes with a trowel about 15cm deep and 30cm apart. Put compost in the bottom of the hole or trench. Plant one seed potato with sprout side up in each hole, or plant them 30cm apart in the trench, and cover with soil. If you have more than one row, leave 45cm between the rows. You can also plant potatoes singly in amongst your flowers, but you

Chitting potatoes.

Planting potatoes.

need to allow enough room round the plant to earth it up (see below). Don't forget to label them! **In containers,** put 10cm of compost or soil, or a mix of the two, in the bottom, place seed potatoes 15-20cm apart on top, and cover with another 10cm of compost or soil.

How do potatoes grow?

Potatoes grow leaves above the earth and later on produce flowers, which sometimes turn into a green fruit – don't eat these, they are poisonous! The potatoes grow on the roots of the plant under the earth.

Looking after your potatoes

Earth up: Cover the whole plant with earth once the leaves are about 10cm long. If in the ground, pull up the earth from either side of the row to make a ridge, and do this again when the leaves reappear. For containers, simply add another 10cm of compost or soil to cover; repeat this process until you are near the top of the container. Take care to keep potatoes under the ground – if exposed to the air they turn green and poisonous.

Look out for: Blight (see page 130).

Harvesting

When: About 13-14 weeks from planting – June or July. Potatoes can be harvested as you need them; they are ready when the plants are flowering and the leaves start to die back.

How: Carefully dig the plant up with a fork, or pull the plant out of the container; there will be potatoes on the stems and in the soil – exciting!

Now what?

Put the old stems and leaves on the compost or in your recycling bin and prepare the ground for your next crop (which should not be potatoes).

Potato flowers.

✸ Store your spuds in a cool dark place in a paper sack – keeping them out of the light stops them going green.

Purple sprouting broccoli

Purple sprouting broccoli is a great plant to grow because it provides fresh greens between February and May, at a time when little else is growing. It's expensive to buy as it has a short shelf life. Delicious – our favourite winter veg.

Plant or seed?
Seeds are cheap and easy to grow, but you can also buy plants if you prefer. Half a dozen plants will give you plenty to eat throughout the winter if you have the space. Buy short plants rather than long-legged creatures. 'Early Purple Sprouting' is a popular variety.

Sowing seeds
When and where: From late April to June in pots, modules or a seedbed.
How: Sow the seeds as thinly as possible just beneath the soil, or two seeds per small pot or module, before transplanting to their final homes when the plants are about 10cm tall.

Planting plants
When and where: June–July. Choose a spot that will get some sun during the depth of the winter, but avoid planting in the same place as last year to avoid the build-up of disease.
How: Dig holes about 60cm apart, big enough to take both plant and soil. Dig up the plants you have

Tray of young broccoli plants.

grown from seed by loosening the earth round them with a small fork and digging gently underneath the roots to remove the plant, complete with soil. If they have been grown in small pots, carefully remove them and their soil by turning the pots upside down and tapping gently. Carefully tease apart the roots of the plants. Put one plant in each hole and bury roots to the same depth as before. Press down gently but firmly to secure the plant and water it in.

If you want to grow in a container you will need a large one with some stones in the bottom for drainage. Fill it with soil or compost, plant as above in the centre of the container and put it in a sheltered, sunny position.

How does purple sprouting broccoli grow?

The plants have cabbage-like leaves and can grow quite tall and large. Early the following year the plant will 'sprout' numerous fresh new flowering shoots, both from the top and where the leaves join the main stem. You eat the budding purple shoots and the tender leaves.

Looking after your purple sprouting broccoli

Water: Water well during the first couple of weeks after transplanting.

Support: These large plants will probably need to be staked in the autumn to prevent them blowing over in the winter storms. Hammer in a stout wooden stick by each plant until it is secure in the soil. Attach the plant stem to the stake using garden twine.

Look out for: Wood pigeons and other birds (see page 130), as they may try to eat the leaves during the winter – protect your broccoli plants by covering them with netting.

Harvesting

Between February and May you can snap off the emerging budding shoots when about 15cm long, before the flowers open. Start by picking the central purple bud – this will encourage the plant to grow additional sprouts. Regular picking encourages more to grow.

Now what?

Once the shoots stop emerging or turn to yellow flowers, pull up the plants, flatten the fibrous main stems with a hammer or similar, or chop them up and put them on the compost heap.

Young purple sprouting broccoli shoots.

✳ If you ever cook too much (very unlikely), put it in the fridge and serve cold with vinaigrette – delicious!

Radishes

Radishes are really easy and very quick to grow. They come in a wide variety of shapes and colours and can be grown in between slower-growing vegetables, as they will be harvested well before the other vegetable is ready.

Plant or seed?

Radishes are grown from seeds; try the round 'Scarlet Globe' or the long 'French Breakfast'.

Sowing seeds

When and where: Sow from March to September outdoors, in the ground or in containers or a window box; radishes like sunshine. You can sow more seed every 3 weeks or so until September to give you a continuous supply.

How: Sow outdoors 1cm deep in a shallow drill as thinly as possible and cover with soil; if planting in the ground, sow in rows 15cm apart. Once seedlings appear, thin to 2.5cm apart. Don't try to replant the thinnings – they won't grow.

How do radishes grow?

The leaves appear very quickly above the ground, and the edible radish grows in the ground with its top peeping through.

Looking after your radishes

Water: Radishes need watering well, especially in dry spells.

Look out for: Flea beetle (see page 131).

Harvesting

When: Some varieties are ready within 30 days of sowing; you will see the radish start to appear slightly above the ground. Harvest it when it is small, the size of a cherry – the bigger it is the hotter and tougher it will be.

How: Grab the leaves at ground level and gently pull the radish out of the soil.

Now what?

Plant some more!

❋ **Try planting a winter variety, e.g. 'Black Spanish Round', in July or August for harvesting from October onwards.**

Runner beans

Runner beans are very easy to grow and great value for money, with loads of beans on each plant, which keep on coming for several weeks if you pick them regularly.

Plant or seed?

Either start your beans off indoors from seed and plant out later, or sow direct into the ground, or take a short cut and buy plants that are ready to go. 'Scarlet Emperor' is popular, or 'Hestia' is a dwarf runner bean that does well in containers.

Sowing seeds

When and where: Sow late April in modules or pots indoors; May or June outdoors in the ground, or in containers as long as the danger of frost is past. Runner beans grow best in sunshine out of the wind. You can sow more seed 3-4 weeks after your first sowing to keep the beans coming into the autumn.

How: Indoors, one seed to a small pot, filled with peat-free compost. Sow 5cm deep, with the seed on its side.

Outdoors, they can be grown up tall canes, sticks, trellis or arches or you can grow them singly wherever you have a space. If sowing in rows, sow one seed 5cm deep either side of each support; stick the supports in the ground about 40cm apart - you can tie the supports up in a variety of ways, from wigwams to tent shapes (see page 68).

Planting plants

When and where: Once your indoor-grown plants are 2-3cm high, and the risk of frost is past in late May / early June. Plant at the same spacing as for seeds.

How: Harden off your indoor-grown plants before planting outside. Make a small hole with a trowel, carefully tip the pot upside down letting the plant hang between your fingers, then put the plant

Runner bean seeds.

upright into the hole and plant to the same depth as before. Firm round the stem and water in.

How do runner beans grow?

Prolifically! The plants will grow 2-3m or more if allowed to. First come the flowers, red or white, which in turn become the edible runner bean pods on the vines.

Looking after your runner beans

Water: Runner beans need regular watering in dry weather once flowers appear – they are quite thirsty.

Weed: Keep the area round the base of the plants free from weeds.

Support: The vines need supporting as they climb up the canes – you may need to tie them in to start with until they get the idea of curling round the support.

Pinch out: Once they have reached the top of the sticks, pinch out the tops of the vines.

Look out for: Slugs (see page 131).

Harvesting

When: From July onwards.

How: Beans can be picked as you want them – the smaller ones are the most tender; if you let them grow too long they become stringy and tough. Regular picking encourages the plant to produce more beans. Hold the stem and gently pull the beans away from it.

Now what?

Pull the plants out of the ground, chop them up and put them on the compost heap, or cut off the stems and leave the roots in the ground.

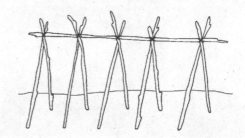

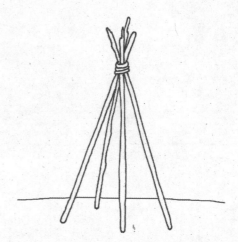

Two methods of support for runner beans.

Runner beans ready to pick.

❋ Save seed by leaving a few pods on the plant until they are crispy and dry. Take the seeds out, put in a warm dry place until completely dry and store somewhere cool and dry until needed.

Salad leaves
'Cut and come again'

Salad leaves come in all shapes, colours and flavours. 'Cut and come again' leaves are easy and quick to grow, and can be sown frequently to give you lots of salad for several months – so much cheaper than salad bags in the shops!

Plant or seed?

If you get a packet of mixed 'cut and come again' leaves it should last you a season if you sow a few every 3 weeks or so. You can choose from a variety of mixtures, or try single varieties such as 'Lamb's Lettuce', 'Bergamo' or the red 'Oak Leaf'. You can buy plants if you want more instant results or have little time to look after your seedlings.

Sowing seeds

When and where: April to September. You can grow and harvest your leaves indoors on a sunny windowsill or you may want to start seeds off indoors before hardening them off and planting outside. **Indoors,** you can sow them in late February/March in containers. **Outdoors,** if you are sowing direct into soil, sow from April onwards. Salad leaves like sun or part shade.

How: Indoors, if you want to raise your own plants, sow thinly in modules or seed trays, covering with a sprinkling of soil. But wait until the weather warms up a little – too early and they won't germinate. **Outdoors,** try to sow seeds as thinly as you can to avoid having to thin them out once they come up. Make a shallow drill about 1cm deep in the soil and sprinkle the seed sparingly into it, covering thinly with soil. Water after sowing.

Planting plants

When and where: Once your plants have several leaves and are big enough to handle, plant outside in the ground 15cm apart with about 25cm between rows. They can be planted between crops that take longer to grow, for example sweetcorn or purple sprouting broccoli, or even in the flowerbed or border. They are ideal for window boxes, pots and growbags on a patio, balcony or windowsill.

How: In the ground, make a hole in the soil with a

❋ You can spice up a salad by growing some hot leaves, like 'Ruby Streaks' mustard or wild rocket (see the following pages).

trowel and carefully put the roots of the plant in, fill the hole with earth and firm gently round its base. Water well.

In a container, put some bits of crockery, flower pot or stone in the bottom of the container for drainage and fill the container with good growing compost. Plant as above.

How do salad leaves grow?

A few small leaves will appear first, which gradually get bigger. Then many new leaves will grow from the centre of the plant.

Looking after your salad leaves

Water: Don't let the plants dry out or they may bolt – water in the early morning if needed.

Weed: Keep the area round the plants free of weeds. You will need to weed frequently, especially when the seedlings are young.

Thin out: You need enough room for your seedlings to flourish, so they will need thinning out – check the seed packet for exact distances.

Look out for: Aphids (see page 130) and slugs (see page 131).

Harvesting

When: From seeds to leaves takes around 3-4 weeks. You can pick a few baby leaves once they are big enough to do so, or leave them to grow a bit more if you want larger leaves.

How: Keep harvesting a few leaves from each plant as they get big enough. For non-stop salad, harvest just the outside leaves, by gently twisting them away from the plant, which will grow more leaves within a few days.

Now what?

You can sow or plant some more seeds at 3-weekly intervals, right through until September. Once the plants start to go to seed, pull them up and put on the compost heap.

'Ruby Streaks' mustard

This beautiful red salad plant has hot peppery leaves that can be added to a bowl of salad leaves, or the larger ones can be stir-fried. It is easy and quick to grow as a cut-and-come-again crop, either in the ground or in containers.

You can plant these leaves outdoors in succession every 3 weeks or so between May and August and harvest from late May to November. Sow thinly in rows 20cm apart and cover with a layer of fine soil. Firm in gently and water. When plants are large

✱ **Unless you like really hot salad you may want to add just a few of these mustard leaves to your salad bowl!**

enough, thin out to about 20cm apart or, if growing in containers, 5cm is enough. Pick leaves as needed, starting with the largest outside ones.

The plants have fine serrated purple leaves and can reach 30cm high or more. Keep an eye out for slugs.

Wild rocket

This popular leaf is a perennial and is really easy to grow. It can be used as a cut-and-come-again plant – harvest it when the leaves are young and it will regrow. A few of its narrow dark green leaves will pep up a salad or a pizza. The leaves get more pungent later in the season.

Sow seed thinly outdoors from April onwards, covering with a thin sprinkling of soil, and thin out to about 20cm apart when plants are big enough to handle. Water in very dry weather; otherwise it just looks after itself. Once it is big enough you can harvest it throughout the growing season – depending on how big you like your leaves. The more you pick, the more it grows.

You many get tiny holes in the leaves from flea beetle (see page 131), but don't worry, they won't affect the flavour.

Once your rocket starts to produce yellow flowers, cut them off to prevent the plant seeding if you don't want it all over your garden. It's not called 'wild' rocket for nothing!

New spring growth from last year's plants.

If you want a broader-leaved rocket with a milder taste, try salad rocket.

Spring onions

Spring onions are extremely easy to grow – they develop quickly and are very productive, take up very little space and can be harvested as needed.

Plant or seed?

Spring onions have to be grown from seed – if you purchased them as plants you would be buying spring onions! 'White Lisbon' is the one to go for.

Sowing seeds

When and where: Sow seeds from March to July. The earlier you sow, the sooner you'll harvest them.
How: Sow seeds very thinly just beneath the soil, either in rows about 15cm apart or as a block. Put them on the soil surface and cover with a light scattering of compost or soil.

How do spring onions grow?

Spring onions produce green leaves about 15cm tall with a white base and a small bulb that is just beneath the surface of the soil. You can eat the lot, green bits and all.

Looking after your spring onions

Water: The seeds and young onions need watering in dry weather. Those grown in containers will need regular watering – probably daily during hot summer months.
Weed: As with most seeds, they will need weeding – but this is relatively simple to do as the onions show themselves quite soon after planting.
Thin out: Harvest some onions early to leave the others about 3cm apart. Don't keep them in the ground growing for too long as they will start to get tough to eat and will develop a large bulb in the soil – they are starting to grow into a 'real' onion!

Harvesting

When: 8-10 weeks from planting. The whole plant can be harvested and eaten. You can pull the onions up as soon as you can see them, but it's best to wait until they are bigger.
How: Hold the plant gently at the base of the leaves and pull the whole onion out of the soil. If your soil is hard, loosen with a trowel or a small fork.

Now what?

Sow some more seeds before the end of July.

✳ **If you plant onion seeds every 3-4 weeks from March to July you will have a succession of fresh green spring onions right through the summer months.**

Sweetcorn

Sweetcorn cooked and eaten immediately after picking tastes fantastic – much sweeter than shop-bought corn. It's a great plant to grow and doesn't need much attention.

Plant or seed?

Sweetcorn is easy to grow from seed, but you can buy plants if you want to take a short cut. Try the very sweet 'Sweet Nugget', or 'Minipop' for smaller cobs for stir-frying.

Sowing seeds

When and where: Sow indoors, early May; outdoors at the end of May in the ground, provided it is not too cold. Sweetcorn likes a sheltered sunny spot.
How: Indoors, sow one seed to a small pot, 2-5cm deep, filled with peat-free compost.
Outdoors, sow 2-5cm deep and 35-45cm apart, in blocks (they grow best this way) or in rows.

Planting plants

When and where: Early June, in the sun.
How: Harden off your indoor-grown plants before planting outside. Plant in blocks, as for seeds. Make a hole with a trowel and put the plant in, to the same depth as before. Firm round the base of the plant and water in.

How does sweetcorn grow?

Sweetcorn can grow up to 2m high before producing flowers that turn into cobs, with tassels on top. The cobs grow from the main stem – usually 2 or 3 to a plant – and are covered with a greenish husk that protects the yellow corn underneath.

Looking after your sweetcorn

Look out for: Birds (see page 130).

Harvesting

When: From August onwards, when the tassels at the top of the plant have turned brown. You can test to see if the cob is ripe by peeling back the protective sheath and pricking one of the corn kernels with a knife – milky juice means it is ripe.
How: Harvest carefully, by holding the main stem and cutting or twisting the husk away from it.

Now what?

Pull out the old plants and chop them up before adding to your compost.

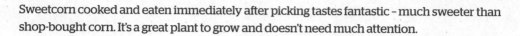

❋ **You can grow courgettes or squash in between your sweetcorn plants, which will help keep the weeds down and make the most of your space.**

Tomatoes

The wonderful thing about growing your own tomatoes is the smell and taste of them when freshly picked. Be prepared to be amazed – they are sweet and incredibly tasty – so different from those in the shops.

Plant or seed?

Both seeds and plants can be used – buy different varieties according to where you want to grow them. **For containers indoors and out,** try 'Gardener's Delight' or any other 'cherry' tomato. **For hanging baskets,** try 'Tumbling Tom', or 'Hundreds and Thousands'. **In the garden,** try 'Alfresco' or 'The

Amateur'. If buying plants, look for short ones with thick stems and dark green leaves in early June.

Sowing seeds

When and where: Plant indoors somewhere with continuous warmth, for example on a south-facing windowsill, in March or April (an airing cupboard will probably be too hot).

How: Sow in small pots or modules, one seed per pot at the depth specified on the packet; keep compost damp but not wet. Cover with a clear plastic lid or cling film to maintain warmth and moisture. When the seedlings start to appear they require lots of sunshine. Remove the lid or cling film before the leaves touch it. When roots start growing through the base of the pot, transplant into pots of about 15cm diameter half full of fresh compost. Remove the fragile plant from its pot very carefully with a spoon or similar and avoid touching it as far as possible. Place the roots into the half-filled larger pot, fill in with more compost

Tomato seedlings.

and gently firm down. Water well, keep the compost damp, and keep in a warm spot until the tomato is ready to be planted into its final home.

Planting plants

When and where: Early June, in a sunny and sheltered spot.

How: Hold the stem gently at soil level and carefully pull both plant and soil out of the pot, turning the pot upside down if necessary. Dig a hole and plant slightly deeper than before – new roots will grow out of the stem below soil level and help make the plant stronger. Press down gently but firmly and water in. Allow about 50cm between plants. If you're planting in a container or hanging basket, fill it with compost and plant as above in the centre of the container, ensuring adequate drainage. Place in a sheltered, sunny position.

How do tomatoes grow?

Upright varieties grow to about 2m, producing clusters of yellow flowers at regular intervals branching out from the main stem; these flowers then become tomatoes.

Hanging basket varieties trail over the edge of the basket, producing flowers and fruit in a similar way.

Looking after your tomatoes

Water: Tomato plants need regular watering, especially when fruiting. Keep the soil damp, not wet. Water the soil, not the leaves.

Support: Upright varieties need additional support. Carefully tie stems to a cane stuck into the soil.

Pinch out: Side shoots that develop need to be 'pinched out' (see below). They grow at the junction between the main leaves and the stem and need removing by pinching between finger and thumb.

Look out for: Slugs and snails (see page 131). Hanging baskets should stay free of them unless the snails drop off trees!

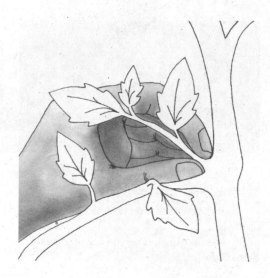

Pinching out.

Tomatoes in a hanging basket.

Harvesting

When: Pick when fruit are bright red, from August onwards.

How: Hold the plant just behind the tomato and twist off the fruit.

Now what?

When fruit is no longer ripening, remove the remaining green tomatoes for cooking. Pull up the plants and put them on the compost heap.

✹ **Green tomatoes can be cooked in many ways – for example in stews, lasagne or chutneys.**

Turnips

Turnips are easy to grow and quick to mature. They provide a tasty and versatile crop early in the year and you can also eat their green leaves. Pop some seeds in the soil and harvest the turnips while they're still small – delicious!

Plant or seed?

Seed only, but they are up before you know it. Try 'Snowdrop' or 'Purple Top Milan'.

Sowing seeds

When and where: Sow your seeds anytime from April through to August, in a nice sunny spot to encourage them to pop up even more quickly.

How: Sow thinly, about 1cm deep, either in rows 25cm apart or in groups, depending on how much space you have.

How do turnips grow?

Turnips grow fast – so stand back and get ready to eat them! Leaves appear above the ground while the edible root in the soil swells up until it's ready for you to harvest. The root colour depends upon which variety you're growing – the name is generally a bit of a giveaway.

Looking after your turnips

Water: They grow well in moist soil, so ideally water daily.

Weed: Keep them weed-free if possible; they're easy to weed as the turnip leaves show themselves early on.

Thin out: Thin the young turnips out to about 10cm apart.

Look out for: Flea beetle (see page 131).

Turnip ready to pick.

Young turnips.

Harvesting

When: 12-14 weeks from sowing. Harvest as soon as they're big enough to eat – probably about golf ball size. You can see how big they are as the top of the swollen root is visible above the soil. Don't leave them in the soil for too long as they will tend to get rather tough.

How: Grasp the base of the leaves and pull the turnip out of the soil.

Now what?

Strange but true, turnips are part of the cabbage family – so when you've pulled up all your turnips use this space for planting anything but members of the cabbage family (including more turnips!).

✲ **Pick them when they're small, and try cooking and eating the young leaves, they're really nice – cook them as you would cabbage leaves. You should be able to get a good picking of these greens when you first thin out the young turnips.**

Chapter 4

Easy-to-grow fruit

Blackberries

Cultivated blackberries are a great fruit for almost any garden – a plant can be squeezed into the smallest sunny corner and can easily be trained to grow up a fence or wall. Unlike their wild cousins, cultivated blackberries include thornless varieties, making them much easier to pick!

Plant or seed?

Plants only. If possible choose plants that are certified to be of healthy, virus-free stock. 'Merton Thornless' is a great variety to buy. Don't be tempted to plant 'Himalaya Giant' unless you have loads of space – it grows rampantly and will soon take over your entire garden!

Planting plants

When and where: Plant out in November or until early December, but not if the soil is frozen. If you're too late, wait till early spring (late March/April). Try to find a sheltered sunny spot: you can plant your blackberry right next to a wall or fence and train the plant to grow up this.

How: Remember that these bushes will be growing in this spot for some time, so prepare the ground well. Dig thoroughly to get rid of all weeds and mix in some compost and/or well-rotted manure. Plant shallowly, spreading out the roots into a wide hole, burying them about 12cm deep before firming down the soil. Then shorten all the shoots to about 25cm long. If planting more than one, keep them about 2.5m apart.

Blackberries need to climb and require horizontal wires about 30cm apart, with the lowest starting about 90cm off the ground. Make these good and strong: they will be supporting quite a lot of weight.

Newly planted blackberries.

How do blackberries grow?

Blackberries fruit on one-year-old shoots, so don't expect any fruit in the first year. Your new plants will produce plenty of long shoots with many leaves; in the second year, flowers appear that turn into your blackberries.

Looking after your blackberries

Support: The shoots produced will need to be trained on to your wires. Tie and/or twist the shoots to the left and right of the plant in the first year of growth - these will be the fruiting canes next year. The following year, let the new shoots grow up centrally, while the previous year's canes will be providing your fruit.

Look out for: For some reason birds do not normally steal blackberries, so hopefully no netting will be necessary.

Prune: After harvesting your fruit, cut the canes that bore fruit down to ground level. Train the new shoots of that year, which are growing centrally, into the same positions as those fruiting shoots you have just cut down. These will become the fruiting shoots for next year.

Harvesting

When: Pick during August and September when the fruits are ripe. Expect to get very purple fingers!
How: Carefully! Mind your fingers - unless you have a thornless variety.

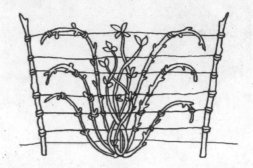

Training blackberry shoots.

Now what?

Retrain the new growth to replace those that have just fruited and been cut back (see 'Prune', left). Feed well every winter/spring by mulching heavily around the base of the plants with compost and/or grass cuttings. These will also keep the weeds down and save you work in the spring.

Blackberry flowers.

✳ To get more blackberry plants, in the summer bend over the tip of a vigorous young shoot and bury it in a hole about 10cm deep, firming down the soil well. The following late autumn/winter separate it from the mother plant by cutting the old stem close to the now-rooted new plant. Transplant the new plant to its final growing position in the spring.

Blackcurrants and redcurrants

Blackcurrants and redcurrants are prolific croppers, providing tasty vitamin-packed fresh fruit for 12-15 years. They will fit into the smallest garden and require very little looking after. They're great fresh, freeze well and make great jam – should you have any left over.

Plant or seed?

Plants only - be patient, they will not crop during their first year. For blackcurrants, try to find 'Ben More' or 'Ben Lomond', while for redcurrants 'Stanza' is really popular.

Planting plants

When and where: Buy the bushes ready to plant in late autumn – November is ideal but early December is still OK, providing the ground is not frozen.

How: Choose a sheltered sunny spot, although they will tolerate a little shade, but avoid wet, poorly drained sites. Prepare the ground really well – your plants could be growing here for the next 15 years! Dig the soil thoroughly, ensuring you remove all weeds and their roots, and incorporate plenty of well-rotted manure and/or compost. Plant the young bushes about 1.5m apart each way (they will look very lonely to start with!) and firm the soil down well.

Then, for blackcurrants, cut all the stems right down to a couple of buds above soil level (use sharp secateurs and cut at a slight angle).

Pruning blackcurrants after planting.

For redcurrants, remove any side shoots growing within 10cm of the soil, cutting them off flush to the main stem. Shorten the remaining shoots by half, cutting just above an outward-facing or upward-facing bud.

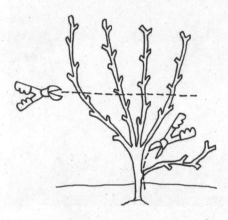
Pruning redcurrants after planting.

How do blackcurrants and redcurrants grow?

Both red and blackcurrants will not fruit during the first year, but they will produce a number of fresh new shoots with many leaves. With regular winter pruning (see box) the bushes will develop into plants about 1.2m in height. The following year the bushes produce new shoots and flowers that become the currants.

Looking after your blackcurrants and redcurrants

Look out for: Birds adore both the developing buds and the fruit, so some form of netting is generally required to protect your crop (see page 130). Ignore this at your peril!

Pruning blackcurrants

First winter (approx. 1 year after planting): Remove any weak shoots and those pointing downwards by cutting with sharp secateurs to about 3cm above soil level. Aim to be left with 6-8 strong shoots.

Second and all other winters: Repeat as for first winter for all new growth. With the remaining older shoots (which have just fruited), cut back to a couple of buds above soil level. In practice, many people adopt the much simpler method of cutting out the old shoots, which the fruit was hanging on, immediately after picking.

Pruning redcurrants

Every winter: Cut back the main shoots to about half of their length, ideally above an outward-facing bud. When the main shoots produce side shoots, cut these right back, leaving just a couple of buds.

Every summer – about July: Cut back all side shoots to about 5 leaves.

Prune: Both red and blackcurrants require pruning (cutting back of some of the shoots) each winter to ensure optimum fruiting.

Harvesting

When: The fruit will be ready to pick in July. Try to wait a week or so after they turn the appropriate

Blackcurrants ready to harvest.

colour before harvesting – they will taste all the better for it.

How: Pick the fruit with the aid of a pair of scissors, cutting off the whole fruiting bunch and sorting them out in the kitchen later.

Now what?
Currants have a lot of roots near the soil surface, so they will benefit from mulching every spring with good compost, followed by grass cuttings later. Remember they are taking their nutrients from this space for 10-15 years – feed them well every spring.

❋ **Additional bushes can be grown by cutting off some young shoots in the autumn, about 30-40cm long, and pushing them halfway down into moist soil. You will be able to see the following summer which ones produce leaves and thrive. Dig these up in the autumn and transplant them to where you want your new bushes to grow.**

Blueberries

Blueberries are a delicious 'superfood' that can be expensive in the shops. Growing your own means you will have really tasty, unsprayed fruit that has not journeyed miles to your plate.

Plant or seed?

Buy blueberry bushes – they are not cheap, but as they are perennial plants that live for up to 20 years you will only have to invest in them once. Try 'Bluecrop' or 'Bluegold'.

Planting plants

When and where: Plant between November and March outdoors in a sunny, sheltered site.
As blueberries need an acid soil to thrive, it is best to grow them in containers filled with ericaceous compost – a special, slightly acidic compost available from garden centres.
How: Dig a hole large enough to accommodate your blueberry plant up to the level of soil of the pot it came in. Pop the plant in the hole and fill it with ericaceous compost, firming carefully round the base of the plant.

How do blueberries grow?

Blueberries produce white flowers which then turn into blueberries. Young plants will yield less fruit than more mature ones, and to get a good crop you probably need more than one bush.

Looking after your blueberries

Feed: Blueberries benefit from feeding with ericaceous fertiliser.
Look out for: Birds (see page 130) – protect fruit with netting once the berries start to form.

Harvesting

When: Between July and September, when the berries plump up and turn a rich blue. Try pulling them away from the stem – if they come away easily, they're ready.
How: Gently pull the berries away from the plant, taking care not to bruise them.

Now what?

Prune in winter. Remove any stems that are broken or diseased, or older branches that no longer produce much fruit, by cutting with sharp secateurs to within 10cm of the main stem.

✸ **Blueberries prefer rainwater – so it's handy to have a water butt to collect it.**

Raspberries

Raspberries are easy to grow, produce a lot of fruit and, if you have room for both summer-fruiting and autumn-fruiting varieties, you will have fruit from July to October. Our favourite – there's nothing like fresh-picked raspberries for breakfast!

Plant or seed?

Raspberries are sold as plants that have a number of short canes about 15cm high when you buy them. Try 'Malling Jewel' for summer and 'Autumn Bliss' for autumn.

Planting canes

When and where: Canes can be planted between November and March and grow best in a sunny, sheltered spot, out of the wind.

How: The growing canes will need support. Put a post at each end of the row and string wires at 30cm intervals between them. As the canes grow up, tie them into the wires for support. Plant canes about 5-8cm deep, 40cm apart in rows, leaving 1.5m between rows. Firm them in gently and water, tying in any that are long enough to the first wire. You can also grow them singly in containers, providing the container is big enough (35-40cm diameter is OK) and you can support the developing cane, or pop one or two in your flower garden, with a bamboo cane to support them.

How do raspberries grow?

Raspberry canes grow from early spring to summer or autumn, depending on the type, with leaves

Newly planted raspberry cane.

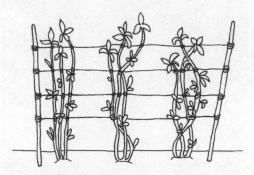

Supported raspberry canes.

Pruning summer raspberries

Once you have harvested your raspberries, cut the canes that had fruit on them down to the ground and tie in the soft canes that did not fruit this year. New fruit will grow on these canes next year.

Pruning autumn raspberries

Cut canes to about 15cm above the ground in February or early March. They will grow big enough to bear fruit again by the following autumn.

appearing first, followed by white flowers, which then become raspberries. Raspberries start off as hard yellowy-green berries and then ripen to full-flavoured, deep red, soft fruit.

Looking after your raspberries

Water: Regular watering is necessary in dry weather once flowers appear.

Weed: Keep the soil free of weeds.

Support: Tie the canes to the supporting wires as they grow.

Feed: If you are growing in containers, it is a good idea to feed the raspberries with a good liquid feed in the growing season.

Look out for: Birds (see page 130) - protect with netting if you don't want to lose your crop!

Harvesting

When: Summer varieties: July and August.
Autumn varieties: late July to October.
How: Once the berries have turned from gold to a deep red, pull them gently from the hull that they are attached to, trying not to squash them. The best time to harvest is on a dry day. If you leave them on the cane when it is wet you run the risk of them going mouldy.

Now what?

Weed round the base of the canes after pruning.

Raspberry flowers, and fruits starting to form.

❋ **Raspberries freeze well – lay them on a baking tray and freeze separately before putting into containers in the freezer.**

Rhubarb

Rhubarb is a joy to have in the garden: it requires very little attention, tends to be trouble-free, and comes up quietly year after year.

Plant or seed?

Rhubarb comes as 'crowns' (chunks of root), usually available in November. Maybe friends or neighbours are dividing their rhubarb plants and can give you a couple of crowns to get you started? Try 'Victoria' or 'Glaskins Perpetual', a quick-growing variety.

Planting crowns

When and where: Between October and March. Rhubarb doesn't need a lot of sun to thrive, so a damp, semi-shaded spot is fine.

How: Plant with the bud just peeping through the surface of the soil, leaving 90cm between each plant. You could put a couple of individual plants in the flowerbed, but if you don't want to crowd your flowers, allow plenty of space round them – some plants get as big as 2m across.

How does rhubarb grow?

Each March or April you will see pale pink buds on the crowns above the soil; these gradually turn into long, thick edible stems with very large, inedible, deep green leaves.

Looking after your rhubarb

Mulch: Add a layer of compost or well-rotted manure in winter and clear any dead leaves away from the base, before the plant starts to grow again in spring.

Rhubarb grows well in shade.

A new rhubarb bud.

Harvesting

When: From April onwards. You can pick rhubarb when it is still quite small or let it grow taller - but if you leave it to grow too big it will not have such a good flavour or texture.

How: Hold the stalk firmly at its base and pull gently. Take only a couple of stalks from each plant, leaving some to die back, so that you don't sap the plant of its strength.

Now what?

Dividing crowns: You can divide your crowns every 5 or 6 years if you want more plants or gifts for friends. In December, carefully lift the plant with a fork and then take a sharp spade and slice through the middle - you now have two rhubarb crowns to plant. You can take smaller slices to make more new crowns if you want.

✳ **Avoid cooking in aluminium pots (rhubarb corrodes it). Rhubarb is delicious if baked in a little water with brown sugar and chopped ginger. But don't eat the leaves – they are toxic!**

Chapter 5

Easy-to-grow herbs

Basil

It is easy to have a love affair with this wonderful herb, and you can use it with many meals during the summer months. The wonderful thing about basil is that the more you pick, the more it grows.

Plant or seed?

The choice is yours, but if growing from seed you will need to give the seedlings a little loving care. Try growing 'Sweet Basil' and 'Purple Basil', but there are many more varieties to try if you feel adventurous. If you are buying plants, look for short, healthy plants with thick stems in early June.

Sowing seeds

When and where: Plant indoors somewhere with continuous warmth in March/April. An airing cupboard will probably be too hot.

How: Sow one seed per small pot, or thinly in trays, at the depth specified on the packet; keep the compost damp but not wet. Cover with a clear plastic lid or cling film. When seedlings start to appear they require lots of sunshine. Remove the plastic cover before the leaves touch it. When plants have about four leaves, transplant into pots of about 15cm diameter. Half fill the pot with compost, extract the fragile plant with a spoon or similar and avoid touching it. Place the ball of roots into the half-filled larger pot, fill in with more compost and gently firm down. Water well, keep warm and keep the compost damp until the basil is planted into its final home in early June.

Planting plants

When and where: Be patient and wait until all risk of frost has passed - plants can go in the ground

Basil seedlings.

from early June. Basil is a plant that will not grow outdoors in the UK unless you can provide it with a warm, sunny and sheltered spot. If this is simply not possible, grow it indoors on a sunny windowsill.

How: Hold the stem of the plant gently at soil level and gently pull both plant and soil out of the pot, turning the pot upside down if necessary. Dig a hole and plant your basil to same soil level as before. Fill the hole with soil and press down gently but firmly to secure the plant, then water in. Allow about 30cm between plants. If planting in a container, fill it with compost and plant several plants as above in the centre of the container, ensuring adequate drainage. Place in a sheltered, sunny position.

How does basil grow?

Initially, basil grows on one central stem. However, when the plant is growing vigorously and is about 10-15cm high, cut the growing tip off to use. This enables the basil plant to branch out from this point, producing many more shoots. Continue to do this whenever fresh shoots are large enough. This will eventually produce a large, bushy and very productive basil plant of about 50cm in height. If you don't pick the growing tips off, the plant will flower and cease to be productive.

Looking after your basil

Water: Indoors, water about every other day. **Outdoors,** basil only needs watering in very dry conditions.

Harvesting

When: From the end of June.
How: Pick off growing tips complete with leaves when required, as described above. The more you pick, the more you get – what a good arrangement!

Now what?

Basil plants growing indoors will continue to grow throughout the winter if you look after them. If you cut down outdoor plants to just above soil level before the frosts arrive, transplant them into a pot and bring indoors on to a warm, sunny windowsill. The transplanted plants will probably send up fresh shoots to keep you going into the winter.

Basil ready to pick.

Red basil.

✸ **Make pesto with your excess basil leaves, to freeze and use throughout the winter. We freeze it in ice-cube trays and then transfer when frozen into plastic bags.**

Mint

If you have any garden space at all, grow some mint. It's so easy to grow, smells wonderful whenever you touch it and is just great for cooking in a wide range of dishes, from new potatoes to mint sauce.

Plant or seed?

Mint is so easy to grow from splitting an existing plant that seeds are never used. Ready-potted plants can be purchased from April onwards. The most common by far is 'Spearmint', which is our favourite.

Planting plants

When and where: Mint is such a hardy herb that you can plant it at any time of the year, provided the ground is not frozen, and it will reappear year after year. It will grow in most situations, providing it has some sunshine during the day.

How: To plant out, simply dig a hole large enough for the roots of your plant, place the roots in the hole, cover with soil and firm down. Water in well. If you don't want it to spread, plant in a container.

How does mint grow?

Mint throws up lots of stems from its roots. The leaves, which are the part to use and eat, start appearing from the end of April onwards and continue until autumn. Cutting the ends off the shoots will encourage many more shoots and discourage the plant from producing flowers. If these do appear, cut them off as soon as possible to encourage further leaf production.

Looking after your mint

Water: Mint thrives with plenty of watering.

Harvesting

When: As soon as the young leaves appear, from the end of April until October.

How: Cut off the leaves and shoots with scissors as and when needed, as described above. The young tender leaves are best to use in salads, with the tougher leaves used as flavouring for cooked food.

Now what?

Wash your mint and freeze in a plastic bag for winter use.

✸ **Chop out a bit of mint root with a spade, plant in a pot and keep indoors on a sunny windowsill for early mint next year.**

Parsley

Parsley is bursting with vitamins and can be used in many dishes. Grow some on your kitchen windowsill or just outside your back door, and keep the scissors handy.

Plant or seed?

You can grow parsley from seed – it takes a long time to germinate and is best started off indoors – but if you want the quick route you can buy plants and grow them in containers, either inside on your windowsill or outside, or in the ground. Try 'Champion Moss Curled', or a flat-leaved variety like 'Italian Giant'.

Sowing seeds

When and where: **Indoors,** sow in March/April on a sunny windowsill.

Outdoors, sow in May in a sunny spot and again in August for a second crop.

How: Sow as thinly as possible in pots or modules, 1cm deep, and cover with a clear plastic lid or cling film. Water in well and don't let your seedlings get too dry. Parsley can take 4-6 weeks before it germinates and another 6 weeks before it is ready to eat – be patient! Eventually, small seedlings will appear with delicate leaves. Once big enough to handle they can be split up and planted into other pots or containers, or, after hardening off, outside.

Planting plants

When and where: Plant your seedlings out when the risk of frost is past in early June, in a sunny spot.

How: Carefully separate your seedlings with a small spoon or similar, avoiding touching the roots if possible. Dig a small hole with trowel and drop the root of the seedling into it, filling in the hole

Parsley seedlings.

Flat-leaved parsley.

Looking after your parsley
Water: Parsley needs lots of water to thrive.
Weed: Keep the plants clear of weeds.
Look out for: Slugs (see page 131) when the seedlings are young.

Harvesting
When: As you need it, once there are enough leaves on the stalks for you to use.
How: Cut each stalk of parsley at its base, starting with the outside stalks. It will keep in a jar in water for several days.

You can store parsley by washing and popping it in a plastic bag in the freezer or cutting it up and freezing it in water in ice-cube trays for using in winter.

Now what?
Sow more seed each month and you will have parsley through to late autumn. Leave the old plants in the ground throughout the winter and if you are lucky they will seed themselves, saving you the effort of sowing more the following year.

with soil and gently firming round each seedling. Space plants or seedlings 20-25cm apart. Water carefully.

How does parsley grow?
First, a seedling appears with tiny leaves on a single stem, which produces many more stems and leaves as the plant gets bigger – you can eat it all.

✷ **If you have plenty of parsley, try making Armenian soup – it's really tasty.**

Parsley ready to use.

Rosemary

Rosemary is an amazing aromatic evergreen plant that just sits there and looks after itself year after year. Plant it just outside the kitchen so that a few sprigs can be cut off at any time.

Plant or seed?

Although you can grow it from seed, this is rarely done because rosemary is so easily grown by breaking off a piece of a friend's plant or by purchasing small plants. Ready-potted plants can be bought from April onwards. The most common variety is *Rosmarinus officinalis*, but if you need a small plant for a container or window box look out for 'Rosemary Capri'.

Planting plants

When and where: April to September. Rosemary prefers a sunny, non-waterlogged spot.
How: Dig a hole, place the roots in it and cover with soil, then firm the soil down and water well. To grow some of your own rosemary from another plant, simply break off a few shoots of about 15-20cm long and stand them in a jar of water. After a couple of weeks, when some roots appear, transplant as above to their permanent position.

How does rosemary grow?

Once your rosemary is established, it will produce numerous fresh shoots throughout the summer months and stay evergreen all year. In spring it produces delightful blue flowers.

Looking after your rosemary

Water: Water for the first few weeks. Once your rosemary gets going it requires very little attention.
Prune: As soon as your plant is large enough for either you or your garden, simply cut back the shoots after they have flowered.

Harvesting

When: April is the best time to harvest, but you can also harvest small sprigs all year round.
How: Cut off the tips with scissors.

Now what?

Leave it alone – it thrives in all but the coldest of winters, and may well survive even those.

✳ **Bunches of rosemary hung around the house smell divine during the winter months. Hang in a warm spot to dry and use for cooking.**

Sage

Sage is an easy-to-grow evergreen. The most common plants have either variegated, grey-green or purple leaves. It grows quite quickly, so you may need to trim it if you haven't got much room.

Plant or seed?

Sage is perennial – buy a sage plant and it will go on for years with very little attention. (It's hardly worth buying seeds – you rarely need more than one plant.) Try the variegated 'Golden Sage', or 'Purple Sage' or 'Green Sage'.

Planting plants

When and where: It's best to buy plants in the spring. Sage thrives in sunshine and it grows well in the ground and in containers, provided they don't get too dry.

How: Dig a hole a bit bigger than the pot your plant comes in, planting to the same depth as before. Firm in round the main stem and water.

How does sage grow?

Sage grows prolifically during the summer months and, as it is evergreen, you will always have leaves to eat from this attractive plant, even in winter.

Looking after your sage

Water: If you are growing it in a container it will need watering in very dry weather.

Weed: Sage tends to cover the ground well, but keep the base of the plant weed-free.

Harvesting

When: You can harvest throughout the year, as you need it.

How: Holding the stem, pick individual leaves or whole sprigs.

Now what?

Hang some up to dry for the days when you don't want to go outside.

When it starts to get straggly, cut it back in spring to the size you want – it gets big quite quickly!

✽ **It is a good idea to replace your sage plant every five years or so, as they tend to get woody.**

Thyme

Thyme is a perennial that comes in many different shapes, colours, sizes and flavours. It is easy to grow, thrives in poor soil and doesn't need much attention.

Plant or seed?

Whilst thyme can be grown from seed, it is easiest to buy plants and have an instant addition to your herb collection. There are many different varieties, for example 'Common Thyme' or 'Doone Valley', a low-growing, variegated variety.

Planting plants

When and where: You can add thyme to your window box, container or garden from April to September. Plant it in a dry, sunny spot – it loves sunshine.
How: Dig a hole a bit bigger than the pot your plant comes in, and plant to the same depth as before. Fill with soil, firm in round the main stem and water.

How does thyme grow?

Plants produce new shoots and leaves in the summer, followed by pink or white flowers.

Looking after your thyme

Water: Thyme is generally maintenance-free, but if you have exceptionally dry weather you may need to water it, especially if it is in a container.
Prune: After the plant has flowered, give it a trim with scissors or shears, cutting back by about 5cm – trimming it will encourage new growth next year.

Harvesting

When: When you need it.
How: Cut off sprigs with scissors to add to stews, sauces and to sprinkle over roast vegetables.

Now what?

Plants may need replacing after a few years if they get woody and stop producing so many leaves.

Thyme in a pot.

A variegated variety of thyme.

❋ If you want more thyme plants, dig the plant up in April and gently pull it apart into several pieces, roots and all. Then put the new plants into pots of compost or in the garden and water in.

Chapter 6

Useful gardening terms

A few basic gardening terms

Annual: A plant that lasts only one year – the majority of vegetables are annuals and need planting every year.

Bed: The area that plants grow in, e.g. flowerbed, asparagus bed, etc.

Bolt: See 'Go to seed'.

Chit: A strange word meaning the process of sprouting seed potatoes to give them a 'kick start'. The seed potatoes are spread out on trays or in egg boxes and put somewhere dry and frost-free, where they sprout before planting.

Cloche: A transparent, normally portable cover put over plants to shelter them from the elements and raise the temperature inside. They are made out of a variety of materials, from purpose-built cloches made of glass or plastic to transparent plastic drinks bottles with their bases cut off, for single plants.

Compost: This word has two different meanings: it's either a growing medium for starting off seeds

Two types of cloche.

Newly germinated seedlings.

and raising plants in, which you normally buy (either 'seed compost' or 'potting compost'), or it's the stuff you can make in a bin outside from kitchen and garden waste, which is used to improve soil. (You can also buy this ready-made.)

Drill: A straight groove made in the soil by a stick or even a finger prior to sowing seeds.

Earth up: Raising the soil level around a plant's base.

Ericaceous compost: A wonderful-sounding name simply meaning a special compost that is slightly acidic. This type of compost is needed for a few plants, such as blueberries.

Firm round or firm down: Gently pressing the soil around the stem of a newly planted seedling or plant to both stabilise it and make it feel at home.

Germinate: The transformation that takes place when a seed changes into a living, growing plant.

Go to seed: What happens to some vegetables (e.g. lettuce) or herbs (e.g. parsley) if they are left too long before harvesting – they go past their tastiest stage and grow flowers that turn to seed.

Grow on: Raising seedlings to a stage when they are big enough to be planted out and fend for themselves.

Harden off: The gradual process of acclimatising your plants to the outside world over several days, by putting them outside during the day and bringing them in at night.

Mulch: Covering the soil with a thin layer of compost, grass cuttings or similar. Mulch is normally put around plants to prevent the soil drying out, to suppress weeds and to increase the soil's fertility. Worms relish pulling the rotting organic matter into the soil.

Perennial: A plant that lives for longer than a couple of seasons, such as raspberries, mint, thyme and rhubarb.

Pinch out: The removal of unwanted side shoots on plants such as tomatoes, or the removal of growing tips of certain plants (such as peas) to encourage them to produce more shoots. This is normally done with a finger and thumb – hence the term!

Plant out: That big moment in a plant's life when it is moved, after hardening off, from its sheltered and cosseted environment to its final growing place.

Prune: The removal of branches, woody side shoots or other unwanted growth to encourage the plant to grow as you want.

Shoots: The fresh, new, young growth emerging from plants.

Successional sowing: Sowing the seeds of quick-growing plants, such as lettuces, every three or four weeks, thereby having a succession of fresh food to harvest throughout the summer.

Tendrils: The long and slender growth on some plants, such as peas, that grips objects and supports the main plant as it grows.

Thin out: The removal of some seedlings from a seedbed, enabling the remainder to have sufficient space to grow successfully.

Transplant: Removing a seedling or plant from where it is growing and replanting it in its final home.

Water in: Giving seeds, seedlings and young plants a thorough watering soon after they have been sown or transplanted. This is preferably achieved by using a small watering can with a fine rose attached, so as not to disturb or wash out the seeds or plants.

Chapter 7

Common problems

Raising healthy crops

You may have years of disease-free growing, or be unlucky with your first attempt. This chapter includes just some methods of dealing with pests and diseases that can affect the fruit and vegetables in this book. But prevention is always better than cure – the following are a few tips to help you keep your crops pest- and disease-free.

Protecting seedlings with netting.

Be vigilant Keep an eye on growing plants – there's no substitute for regular inspection of your crops to make sure no unwanted creatures have set up home. Do a nightly prowl with a torch and bucket if you want to keep slug numbers down, especially when it is wet, when they come out in their droves.

Cleanliness Diseases can come in on the wind, on plants, animals and insects, and also on you. To prevent spreading disease, keep things clean and wash your hands and clothes if you have been handling diseased plants, e.g. blighted ones. Reduce hiding places for slugs and woodlice by getting rid of decaying debris from growing areas.

Crop-friendly insects and birds Some insects, for example ladybirds, hoverflies and lacewings, eat the unwelcome ones. Some birds can eat caterpillars before they have time to grow and shred your broccoli. You can encourage beneficial insects and birds by leaving a bit of your garden wild if you have enough room.

Healthy soil means healthy vegetables. To prevent build-up of diseases, ideally avoid planting the same crop in the same place in the garden each year. Change the compost in your containers if you are going to grow the same thing in them next year.

Netting on hoops to keep the birds off.

Protection Mesh, fleece, netting and plastic bottles are useful protection against pests and diseases as well as harsh winter weather.

Shade and sunshine Make sure you give your plants the best conditions for success – sun-loving plants won't thrive in the shade and vice versa.

Timing It's important to sow and plant at the appropriate times to give your plants the best chance of success.

Watering Watch out for changes in the weather and adjust your watering accordingly. Under-watering results in wilted and ultimately dead crops, and if you overwater container-grown plants you could rot their roots.

Weather Become aware of the changes in weather – for example, don't put plants out too soon if there is still a danger of frost and get your watering can out if you have a dry spell.

The most common pests and diseases

Ants affect plants by mining underneath the roots and killing them off. They can also increase aphid populations. Find the nest and, if it is not near your

Keeping the bugs out with fleece.

plants, pour boiling water over it. If the nest is near your plants, either dig the nest out with a spade and put it elsewhere or try disturbing it on a regular basis.

Aphids are tiny, ant-sized insects that suck life from the plant, curl its leaves and stunt its growth. The most common are blackfly (particularly on broad beans), greenfly (they love salads) and whitefly (which happily munch courgettes, broccoli and tomatoes). Spray them off with a mix of organic washing-up liquid and water (one squirt per 500ml), or simply hose them off.

Birds can be useful for eating insects but they can also steal your fruit, pull up young seedlings and plants (especially onions), and make large holes in lettuce, peas, beans, broccoli or spinach. Protect your plants with netting or fleece.

Blackfly See 'Aphids'.

Blight is a fungus that can arrive on the wind in warm, wet weather. It affects tomatoes and potatoes – their leaves go brown and eventually the plant rots. Remove infected leaves and tomatoes from tomato plants and harvest potatoes as soon as you spot blighted leaves – they won't store.

Caterpillars Butterflies lay eggs on broccoli, spinach and other plants. Net plants with a fine net to keep them from laying their eggs on the leaves, and pick off and destroy any caterpillars – they tend to hide underneath the leaves.

Carrot fly affects carrots and parsnips, particularly in dry weather, resulting in tiny holes in your crop. You can keep the flies out by covering your plants with fleece. Try to minimise disturbance to your plants when you are harvesting – their smell attracts the fly.

Flea beetle makes tiny holes in salad leaves, radishes and turnips, but these don't affect the flavour. If you really want to, you can protect plants by growing under fleece or fine netting.

Frost can destroy young plants. Protect with horticultural fleece if there is a danger of frost and don't be tempted to plant your seeds too early, or harden off seedlings, until you are sure that the frosty nights are over.

Greenfly See 'Aphids'.

Mice particularly enjoy digging out and eating pea and bean seeds. A humane mouse trap is a good start, if you haven't got a cat, or start plants off indoors with a mouse trap nearby.

Pea moth If you discover tiny creamy caterpillars eating your peas inside the pods, pick your peas – hopefully there will be some unspoilt ones still inside the pods.

Slugs and snails will eat most of your vegetables if you let them. You can help keep their numbers down by: clearing away any plant debris or large stones so they have nowhere to hide; collecting them by torchlight, particularly after rain; using copper tape at the base of your plant pots; 'slug pubs' – bowls filled with beer buried to their rims (if you can spare the beer); or putting rough stuff, for example coffee grounds, holly or crushed eggshells, round your plants.

Having caught your slug it's either them or your vegetables – there are many ways of getting rid of them: for example, you can snip them, squash them or drown them – over to you!

Whitefly See 'Aphids'.

Woodlice can feed on seedlings, so keep the soil free of debris so they have no food to attract them to your plants.

Metric-imperial conversions

Centimetres to inches

1cm - 0.4"
2cm - 0.8"
2.5cm - 1"
5cm - 2"
10cm - 4"
15cm - 6"
20cm - 8"
25cm - 10"
30cm - 12"
40cm - 16"
50cm - 20"
75cm - 30"
100cm - 40"

Metres to feet

1m - 3'3"
1.25m - 4' 1"
1.5m - 5'
2m - 6'7"